RED ROSES

There are pretty young women everywhere. And there are young men with nice smiles. In every town, in every city, young men are looking at young women, and young women are smiling at them. They look, they meet, they talk, they laugh . . . happy days, sweet nights – it's love.

Will looks at Anna. She is a pretty young woman, and he wants to meet her. But how? He can hear her guitar, but he cannot find her.

Anna looks at Will. She wants to meet him too. But where is he? She can smell his roses in the elevator, but where does he go?

Anna's friend Vicki wants to help. Will's gran wants to help. But nothing happens. Can Anna find Will? Can Will meet Anna? Is it love?

OXFORD BOOKWORMS LIBRARY

Human Interest

Red Roses

Starter (250 headwords)

For Dominic

CHRISTINE LINDOP

Red Roses

Illustrated by
Gavin Reece

OXFORD UNIVERSITY PRESS

OXFORD
UNIVERSITY PRESS

Great Clarendon Street, Oxford ox2 6dp

Oxford University Press is a department of the University of Oxford.
It furthers the University's objective of excellence in research, scholarship,
and education by publishing worldwide in

Oxford New York

Auckland Cape Town Dar es Salaam Hong Kong Karachi
Kuala Lumpur Madrid Melbourne Mexico City Nairobi
New Delhi Shanghai Taipei Toronto

With offices in

Argentina Austria Brazil Chile Czech Republic France Greece
Guatemala Hungary Italy Japan Poland Portugal Singapore
South Korea Switzerland Thailand Turkey Ukraine Vietnam

OXFORD and OXFORD ENGLISH are registered trade marks of
Oxford University Press in the UK and in certain other countries

ISBN: 978 0 19 423434 4

A complete recording of this Bookworms edition of *Red Roses*
is available.

Printed in China

Word count (main text): 1700

For more information on the Oxford Bookworms Library,
visit www.oup.com/elt/gradedreaders

This book is printed on paper from certified and well-managed sources.

CONTENTS

❧ *1* ❧
White roses

It's August. Anna is playing her guitar on the balcony of her new apartment. 'I like it here,' she thinks.

Then her phone rings. It's her friend Vicki.

'I'm coming now, Anna. It's Grandview Apartments, Charlton, isn't it?'

'That's right. See you soon.'

Anna takes her guitar and goes out of her apartment. She goes down in the elevator and goes outside.

Anna is waiting outside the apartment building.

A young man is walking along the street. He is carrying a bunch of white roses.

Anna looks at them. 'What beautiful roses!' she thinks. Then she looks at the young man. 'He's nice too!' she thinks.

The young man looks at her and smiles, and suddenly Anna's face is pink.

Will is walking along the street, when he sees a young woman with a guitar.

'Hmm – a guitar!' he thinks. 'I must play my guitar more often.'

Then he looks at the young woman.

'She's nice!' he thinks, and he smiles at her.

Anna's face is pink, and she looks away. Will goes into Grandview Apartments.

Just then, Vicki arrives in her car.

'Hello, Anna,' she says. 'Are you OK? Your face is a bit pink. What's the matter?'

'Oh – er – nothing,' says Anna.

They drive away. Vicki talks to Anna, but Anna is thinking about the young man.

'Who is he?' she thinks. 'Does he live in the building? Who are the roses for? His wife? His girlfriend? His mother?'

'Anna? Are you listening?' says Vicki.

'Oh! Sorry, Vicki,' says Anna. Her face is red now.

'What are you thinking about?' says Vicki. 'Tell me!'

'Well, I'm thinking about a bunch of roses,' says Anna. 'And a man.'

'Aha! Who is he?' says Vicki.

'I don't know,' says Anna.

'But I want to know,' she thinks.

Will arrives at his gran's apartment.

'Hello, dear,' she says. 'Oh, you are a good boy. You always bring me roses.'

'Of course,' says Will.

Gran makes Will some coffee. She asks him a question, but Will does not answer.

'Will, are you listening? You're thinking about something, aren't you? What is it?'

'Oh – sorry, Gran. It's – it's not important.'

Later, Will says goodbye to his gran. Then he gets into his car and drives away.

In the car he thinks about the young woman with the guitar.

'Where does she live?' he thinks. 'Does she live in one of the apartments? Or has she got a friend there? How can I meet her? Who is she?'

Five minutes later, Anna and Vicki arrive outside the apartment building.

'Goodnight, Vicki,' says Anna.

'Quick – go inside,' says Vicki. 'Just think – you walk out of the elevator, and there is a young man with a bunch of roses. And he says—'

'Oh be quiet,' laughs Anna. 'See you tomorrow.'

Pink roses

It's September. Will is visiting his gran again.

'It's a lovely day, Will,' she says. 'Let's have our coffee on the balcony.'

Will and his gran are sitting on the balcony in the sun, when suddenly Will hears a guitar.

'Listen!' he says. 'That's a guitar. Where's it coming from?' He stands up and looks around, but he cannot see the guitar.

'Excuse me, Gran,' he says. 'I – er – back soon!' And he runs out of the apartment.

Will runs along the corridor. Where is the guitar? And who is playing it?

He stops outside an apartment and listens. Nothing.

'Perhaps it's outside,' he thinks. 'Perhaps she's on her balcony.'

So he goes down in the elevator and goes outside.

Upstairs, Anna takes her guitar and goes inside. She closes the door to the balcony.

'That's it for today,' she thinks.

Will looks at all the balconies, but he cannot see or hear a guitar.

He goes back to his gran's apartment.

'Are you all right, dear?' she says.

'Yes thanks, Gran,' says Will. 'It's just – oh, it's not important. Well, it is important, but . . .'

And Will tells Gran about the girl with the guitar.

A week later, Anna is coming home. She can see a young man near the apartment building, and he is carrying a bunch of roses – pink roses today. But he is not looking, and he does not see her.

Anna walks more quickly. But when she gets to the building, there is nobody there.

She gets into the elevator. There is nobody in the elevator, but she can smell roses – beautiful pink roses.

One day Anna comes home and finds Gran at the door of the building with a lot of bags.

'Oh, can I help you?' she says. 'Can I carry something?'

'Thank you very much,' says Gran.

At the apartment, Gran says, 'Come in, dear. Would you like some coffee?'

'Oh – that's very nice of you,' says Anna. 'I'm new here, and I don't know anybody in the building.'

'What do you do?' asks Gran.

'I'm a music student,' says Anna.

Gran brings some coffee into the room.

'These are lovely apartments, aren't they?' says Anna.

'Oh yes,' says Gran. 'I like it here very much.' She tells Anna about her apartment, and about Charlton. Later Anna gets up.

'I must go now,' she says. 'Thank you for the coffee.'

'Goodbye, dear,' says Gran, and Anna goes out.

'What a nice girl,' Gran thinks. 'But – just a minute. A music student – perhaps she's the girl with the guitar! I can ask her over one day when Will comes. No I can't – I don't know the number of her apartment!'

Later that week Vicki talks to Anna. 'I'm having a party on Saturday,' she says. 'Can you come?'

'Yes, of course!' says Anna. 'Your parties are always wonderful.'

Vicki calls her brother. 'Come to my party on Saturday, James,' she says, 'and bring some friends.'

On Saturday, James and his friends arrive at Vicki's house.

'Hi, Vicki,' says James. 'Meet my friends. This is Tom, and Daniel – and Will.'

Just then, Vicki's phone rings.

'I'm sorry, Vicki,' says Anna. 'I can't come to your party, because I'm not feeling well.'

'Oh Anna! I'm sorry, too,' says Vicki. 'Well, stay in bed, and get better soon.'

Vicki's party is wonderful. Will meets Natalie, and Jane, and Katie. But he does not meet Anna.

Red roses

Now it's October. Will visits his gran, but he does not see Anna. He walks along the corridor, but he does not hear a guitar.

'Where is she?' he thinks.

Anna visits her family for a week, then she comes back to her apartment. She looks for Will, but she does not see him.

'There are lots of men!' says Vicki, but Anna cannot forget Will.

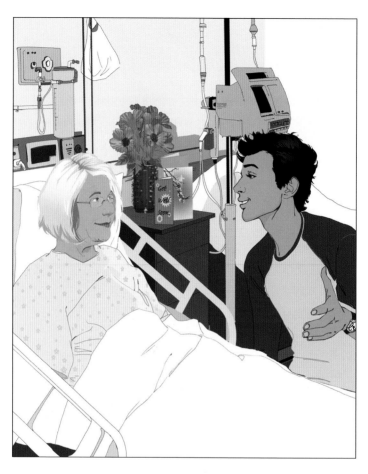

Then Gran goes to hospital for two weeks. One day Will visits her there.

'How are you today, Gran?' he asks.

'Very well thank you, dear. I'm going home on Friday.'

'That's good,' says Will. 'Perhaps I can get some things for you on Thursday and take them to the apartment.'

'That's very nice of you, Will,' says Gran.

After work on Thursday Will goes to the shops and gets some things for Gran. He gets some roses, too, and he puts everything in his car.

Suddenly it begins to rain. Will is getting into his car when he sees his friend Tom.

'Where are you going, Tom?' says Will.

'Home – to Eastfield.'

'I'm going to my gran's apartment in Charlton, so I can take you to Eastfield first.'

'Can you take my friend Anna, too? She's going to Charlton.'

'Yes of course,' says Will.

Tom and Anna get into Will's car.

'Thanks, Will,' says Tom. 'It's not a very nice night!'

'That's all right, Tom,' says Will. He drives Tom home, and then he says to Anna, 'Where are you going, Anna?'

'I'm going to Grandview Apartments. It's on Park Road.'

'That's funny,' says Will. '*I'm* going to Grandview Apartments.'

'Is it her?' he thinks. 'The girl with the guitar?' He looks in the mirror, but he can't see her face very well.

'Can I smell roses?' thinks Anna. 'Is it him – the man with the roses?'

Then they are outside the apartment building. They get out of the car, and then they begin to talk at the same time.

'Oh! It's you!'

'You play the guitar!'

'And you come here with roses!'

'Yes – I always bring roses to my gran.'

'His gran!' thinks Anna. 'Not his wife, not his girlfriend.'

'She's coming home from hospital tomorrow, so I'm taking some things to her apartment,' says Will.

'Can I . . . would you like some help?' says Anna.

'Yes please!' says Will.

They go up to Gran's apartment. Will puts things away, and Anna puts the roses in a vase.

'There – aren't they lovely!' she says. 'I like roses. They smell wonderful.'

'Thank you for your help, Anna,' says Will.

'That's all right,' Anna says. 'Look – would you like to come up to my apartment for coffee?'

'I'd like to very much,' says Will.

He smiles, and she smiles. They go upstairs.

On Friday Gran comes home. Will goes to see her. He is carrying a bunch of red roses.

'That's a big smile, Will!' says Gran. 'Red roses – don't they say "Red roses for love"?'

'Well, Gran . . .' says Will.

Ten minutes later, Will comes out of Gran's apartment and goes upstairs. He's carrying a bunch of red roses.

Gran goes out onto the balcony and sits down in the sun. She can hear a guitar. Then it stops.

Gran hears Will's voice, and Anna's voice. Then Anna laughs.

Gran smiles. She can smell roses – beautiful red roses, in the sun, outside on a balcony.

GLOSSARY

a bit a small amount, not much

along from one end of something to the other end

anybody any person

apartment a group of rooms for living in

around in different places

dear you say this when you speak to someone you like
  or love

funny strange

girlfriend a girl who is a man's special friend

gran grandmother – the mother of your father or
  mother

inside into a room or building

lovely very nice

music what you make when you sing, or play the
  piano, guitar, etc

outside out of a room or building

ring (*v*) make a sound like a bell (e.g. a telephone rings)

smell (*v*) notice something with your nose

upstairs to or in the higher part of a building

voice you speak and sing with your voice

Red Roses

ACTIVITIES

Before Reading

1 **Look at the front and back cover of the book and choose the correct ending for these sentences.**

1 This story is about . . .
  a ☐ work.
  b ☐ love.
  c ☐ families.

2 Roses are . . .
  a ☐ people.
  b ☐ buildings.
  c ☐ flowers.

2 **Guess what happens. In the story . . .**   *Yes*   *No*

		Yes	No
1	Anna and Will never meet.	☐	☐
2	Will meets Vicki.	☐	☐
3	Will takes Anna home in his car.	☐	☐
4	Will meets Anna at work.	☐	☐
5	Anna sees Will on TV.	☐	☐
6	Anna meets Will's grandmother.	☐	☐

While Reading

1 Read pages 1–4, then answer these questions.

1 What does Anna play?
2 Who is coming to her apartment?
3 What colour are Will's roses?
4 Who is Anna thinking about?

2 Read pages 5–8. Are these sentences true (T) or false (F)?

1 Anna is not listening to Vicki.
2 Will always takes apples to Gran.
3 Gran makes coffee for Will.
4 Will talks to Gran about Anna.
5 Anna sees Will outside the apartment building when she comes home.

3 Read pages 9–12, then answer the questions.

Who . . .
1 . . . says: 'It's a lovely day'?
2 . . . runs out of the apartment?
3 . . . closes the door to the balcony?
4 . . . says: 'Are you all right, dear?'?
5 . . . can smell roses in the elevator?

4 Read pages 13–16, then answer these questions.

1 How does Anna help Gran?
2 What is Vicki doing on Saturday?
3 Why does Anna stay at home on Saturday?
4 Who does Will meet at the party?

5 Read pages 17–20, then match the sentence halves to make four complete sentences.

1 Will walks along the corridor . . .
2 Anna visits her family for a week . . .
3 Will is getting into his car . . .
4 Will is going to Charlton . . .

a then she comes back to her apartment.
b so he can take Tom to Eastfield first.
c but he does not hear a guitar.
d when he sees his friend Tom.

6 Read pages 21–24. Are these sentences true (T) or false (F)?

1 Will takes the roses to his mother.
2 Anna puts the roses in a vase.
3 Anna asks Will to her apartment.
4 Will has a bunch of red roses for Gran.
5 Gran laughs when she smells the roses.

After Reading

1 What do you know about Anna? Write a description using these words:

live / Grandview Apartments / Charlton
music student / play guitar
friend / called Vicki
like / help people
like parties / roses

2 Put these sentences in the correct order. Number them 1–10.

a ☐ Tom and Anna get into Will's car.

b ☐ 'Is she the girl with the guitar?' Will thinks.

c ☐ Will goes shopping for Gran.

d ☐ They arrive at the apartment building and get out of the car.

e ☐ Then they go to Anna's apartment.

f ☐ Will drives Tom home.

g ☐ Anna says, 'I'm going to Grandview Apartments.'

h ☐ Anna helps Will with the roses.

i ☐ Then Will and Anna meet!

j ☐ Then he sees his friend Tom.

3 Who says this? Who do they say it to?

1 'I'm thinking about a bunch of roses.'

2 'That's a guitar. Where's it coming from?'

3 'Can I carry something?'

4 'Come to my party on Saturday.'

5 'Stay in bed, and get better soon.'

6 'Can you take my friend Anna, too?'

4 Complete this summary of the story. Use these words:

apartment   because   hears   home
do not   nice   outside   party   rain   red

One day Anna sees Will with a bunch of roses outside her _____ building. She thinks, 'He's _____.' Will likes Anna too, but they _____ meet. Then Will _____ a guitar. Is it Anna's guitar? He goes _____, but he cannot see it.

Anna's friend Vicki asks Anna and Will to her _____, but Anna cannot go _____ she is not well. Then one afternoon Will sees his friend Tom in the _____. He takes Tom and Tom's friend Anna _____. This time, Will and Anna meet. The next day, Will takes a bunch of roses to the apartment building – but they are _____ roses, for Anna.

ABOUT THE AUTHOR

Christine Lindop was born in New Zealand and taught English in France and Spain before settling in Great Britain. She has written more than twenty books, including several Bookworms: *Sally's Phone* (Starter), *Ned Kelly: A True Story* (Stage 1), and *Australia and New Zealand* (Stage 3). She has also adapted *Goldfish* (Stage 3) and edited *A Tangled Web* for the Oxford Bookworms Collection. She has worked on many other Oxford readers series as both an editor and a writer. In her free time she likes reading, watching films, gardening, and cooking.

OXFORD BOOKWORMS LIBRARY

Classics • Crime & Mystery • Factfiles • Fantasy & Horror
Human Interest • Playscripts • Thriller & Adventure
True Stories • World Stories

The OXFORD BOOKWORMS LIBRARY provides enjoyable reading in English, with a wide range of classic and modern fiction, non-fiction, and plays. It includes original and adapted texts in seven carefully graded language stages, which take learners from beginner to advanced level. An overview is given on the next pages.

All Stage 1 titles are available as audio recordings, as well as over eighty other titles from Starter to Stage 6. All Starters and many titles at Stages 1 to 4 are specially recommended for younger learners. Every Bookworm is illustrated, and Starters and Factfiles have full-colour illustrations.

The OXFORD BOOKWORMS LIBRARY also offers extensive support. Each book contains an introduction to the story, notes about the author, a glossary, and activities. Additional resources include tests and worksheets, and answers for these and for the activities in the books. There is advice on running a class library, using audio recordings, and the many ways of using Oxford Bookworms in reading programmes. Resource materials are available on the website <www.oup.com/elt/gradedreaders>.

The *Oxford Bookworms Collection* is a series for advanced learners. It consists of volumes of short stories by well-known authors, both classic and modern. Texts are not abridged or adapted in any way, but carefully selected to be accessible to the advanced student.

You can find details and a full list of titles in the *Oxford Bookworms Library Catalogue* and *Oxford English Language Teaching Catalogues*, and on the website <www.oup.com/elt/gradedreaders>.

THE OXFORD BOOKWORMS LIBRARY
GRADING AND SAMPLE EXTRACTS

STARTER • 250 HEADWORDS

present simple – present continuous – imperative – can/cannot, must – going to (future) – simple gerunds …

Her phone is ringing – but where is it?

Sally gets out of bed and looks in her bag. No phone. She looks under the bed. No phone. Then she looks behind the door. There is her phone. Sally picks up her phone and answers it. ***Sally's Phone***

STAGE 1 • 400 HEADWORDS

… past simple – coordination with and, but, or – subordination with before, after, when, because, so …

I knew him in Persia. He was a famous builder and I worked with him there. For a time I was his friend, but not for long. When he came to Paris, I came after him – I wanted to watch him. He was a very clever, very dangerous man. ***The Phantom of the Opera***

STAGE 2 • 700 HEADWORDS

… present perfect – will (future) – (don't) have to, must not, could – comparison of adjectives – simple if clauses – past continuous – tag questions – ask/tell + infinitive …

While I was writing these words in my diary, I decided what to do. I must try to escape. I shall try to get down the wall outside. The window is high above the ground, but I have to try. I shall take some of the gold with me – if I escape, perhaps it will be helpful later. ***Dracula***

… should, may – present perfect continuous – *used to* – past perfect –
causative – relative clauses – indirect statements …

Of course, it was most important that no one should see Colin, Mary, or Dickon entering the secret garden. So Colin gave orders to the gardeners that they must all keep away from that part of the garden in future. ***The Secret Garden***

STAGE 4 • 1400 HEADWORDS

… past perfect continuous – passive (simple forms) –
would conditional clauses – indirect questions –
relatives with *where/when* – gerunds after prepositions/phrases …

I was glad. Now Hyde could not show his face to the world again. If he did, every honest man in London would be proud to report him to the police. ***Dr Jekyll and Mr Hyde***

STAGE 5 • 1800 HEADWORDS

… future continuous – future perfect –
passive (modals, continuous forms) –
would have conditional clauses – modals + perfect infinitive …

If he had spoken Estella's name, I would have hit him. I was so angry with him, and so depressed about my future, that I could not eat the breakfast. Instead I went straight to the old house. ***Great Expectations***

STAGE 6 • 2500 HEADWORDS

… passive (infinitives, gerunds) – advanced modal meanings –
clauses of concession, condition

When I stepped up to the piano, I was confident. It was as if I knew that the prodigy side of me really did exist. And when I started to play, I was so caught up in how lovely I looked that I didn't worry how I would sound. ***The Joy Luck Club***

Sally's Phone

CHRISTINE LINDOP

Sally is always running – and she has her phone with her all the time: at home, on the train, at work, at lunchtime, and at the shops.

But then one afternoon suddenly she has a different phone . . . and it changes her life.

Star Reporter

JOHN ESCOTT

'There's a new girl in town,' says Joe, and soon Steve is out looking for her. Marietta is easy to find in a small town, but every time he sees her something goes wrong . . . and his day goes from bad to worse.

Ned Kelly: A True Story
CHRISTINE LINDOP

When he was a boy, he was poor and hungry. When he was a young man, he was still poor and still hungry. He learnt how to steal horses, he learnt how to fight, he learnt how to live – outside the law. Australia in the 1870s was a hard, wild place. Rich people had land, poor people didn't. So the rich got richer, and the poor stayed poor.

Some say Ned Kelly was a bad man. Some say he was a good man but the law was bad. This is the true story of Australia's most famous outlaw.

Pocahontas
Retold by Tim Vicary

A beautiful young Indian girl, and a brave Englishman. Black eyes, and blue eyes. A friendly smile, a laugh, a look of love . . . But this is North America in 1607, and love is not easy. The girl is the daughter of King Powhatan, and the Englishman is a white man. And the Indians of Virginia do not want the white men in their beautiful country.

This is the famous story of Pocahontas, and her love for the Englishman John Smith.